RODGERS AND HAMMERSTEIN™

Music by
Richard Rodgers

Book and Lyrics by
Oscar Hammerstein II

Cover Photo: 20th Century Fox/courtesy Everett Collection

ISBN-13: 978-0-88188-089-2
ISBN-10: 0-88188-089-2

WILLIAMSON MUSIC®

A RODGERS AND HAMMERSTEIN COMPANY

www.williamsonmusic.com

Exclusively Distributed By

HAL•LEONARD®
CORPORATION

7777 W. BLUEMOUND RD. P.O. BOX 13819 MILWAUKEE, WI 53213

Visit Hal Leonard Online at
www.halleonard.com

Rodgers and Hammerstein's

The King and I

"THE KING AND I is the essence of musical theater, an occasion when drama, music, dance and decor combine to take the audience on an unforgettable journey."

— *Houston Chronicle*

To learn more about THE KING AND I and the other great musicals available for production through R&H Theatricals, please visit our award-winning website
www.rnhtheatricals.com
or contact

229 W. 28TH ST., 11th FLOOR
NEW YORK, NEW YORK 10001

THEATRICALS

PHONE: (212) 564-4000
FAX: (212) 268-1245
E-MAIL: theatre@rnh.com

All interior photos (unless otherwise noted) provided courtesy of
The Rodgers & Hammerstein Organization

The King and I

CONTENTS

RICHARD RODGERS & OSCAR HAMMERSTEIN II

Rodgers and Hammerstein under the marquee for THE KING AND I (1951)

After long and highly distinguished careers with other collaborators, Richard Rodgers (composer) and Oscar Hammerstein II (librettist/lyricist) joined forces to create the most consistently fruitful and successful partnership in the American musical theatre.

Prior to his work with Hammerstein, Richard Rodgers (1902-1979) collaborated with lyricist Lorenz Hart on a series of musical comedies that epitomized the wit and sophistication of Broadway in its heyday. Prolific on Broadway, in London and in Hollywood from the '20s into the early '40s, Rodgers & Hart wrote more than forty shows and film scores. Among their greatest were ON YOUR TOES, BABES IN ARMS, THE BOYS FROM SYRACUSE, I MARRIED AN ANGEL and PAL JOEY.

Throughout the same era Oscar Hammerstein II (1895-1960) brought new life to a moribund artform: the operetta. His collaborations with such preeminent composers as Rudolf Friml, Sigmund Romberg and Vincent Youmans resulted in such operetta classics as THE DESERT SONG, ROSE-MARIE and THE NEW MOON. With Jerome Kern he wrote SHOW BOAT, the 1927 masterpiece that changed the course of modern musical theatre. His last musical before embarking on an exclusive partnership with Richard Rodgers was CARMEN JONES, the highly-acclaimed 1943 all-black revision of Georges Bizet's tragic opera CARMEN.

OKLAHOMA!, the first Rodgers & Hammerstein musical, was also the first of a new genre, the musical play, representing a unique fusion of Rodgers' musical comedy and Hammerstein's operetta. A milestone in the development of the American musical, it also marked the beginning of the most successful partnership in Broadway musical history, and was followed by CAROUSEL, ALLEGRO, SOUTH PACIFIC, THE KING AND I, ME AND JULIET, PIPE DREAM, FLOWER DRUM SONG and THE SOUND OF MUSIC. Rodgers & Hammerstein wrote one musical specifically for the big screen, STATE FAIR, and one for television, CINDERELLA. Collectively, the Rodgers & Hammerstein musicals earned 35 Tony Awards, 15 Academy Awards, two Pulitzer Prizes,

THE KING AND I received five Tony Awards in 1952, including Best Musical, Best Actress in a Musical (Lawrence) and Best Featured Actor in a Musical (Brynner). From left to right: Oscar Hammerstein II, Gertrude Lawrence, Richard Rodgers, Helen Hayes, Phil Silvers, Judy Garland and Yul Brynner.

33 USA
BROADWAY SONGWRITERS
RODGERS & HAMMERSTEIN
1999

United States postage stamp honoring Rodgers and Hammerstein, issued September 21, 1999.

SOMETHING GOOD
A Broadway Salute to Richard Rodgers on His 100th Birthday

Friday, June 28, 2002
Gershwin Theatre • New York City

two GRAMMY® Awards and two Emmy Awards. In 1998 Rodgers & Hammerstein were cited by *Time* Magazine and CBS News as among the 20 most influential artists of the 20th century, and in 1999 they were jointly commemorated on a U.S. postage stamp.

Despite Hammerstein's death in 1960, Rodgers continued to write for the Broadway stage. His first solo entry, NO STRINGS, earned him two Tony Awards for music and lyrics, and was followed by DO I HEAR A WALTZ?, TWO BY TWO, REX and I REMEMBER MAMA. Richard Rodgers died on December 30, 1979, less than eight months after his last musical opened on Broadway. In March of 1990, Broadway's 46th Street Theatre was renamed The Richard Rodgers Theatre in his honor.

At the turn of the 21st century, the Rodgers and Hammerstein legacy continued to flourish, as marked by the enthusiasm that greeted their Centennials in 1995 and 2002.

In 1995, Hammerstein's centennial was celebrated worldwide with commemorative recordings, books, concerts and an award-winning PBS special, "Some Enchanted Evening." The ultimate tribute came the following season, when he had three musicals playing on Broadway simultaneously: SHOW BOAT (1995 Tony Award winner, Best Musical Revival); THE KING AND I (1996 Tony Award winner, Best Musical Revival); and STATE FAIR (1996 Tony Award nominee for Best Score).

In 2002, the Richard Rodgers Centennial was celebrated around the world, with tributes from Tokyo to London, from the Hollywood Bowl to the White House, featuring six new television specials, museum retrospectives, a dozen new ballets, half a dozen books, new recordings and countless concert and stage productions (including three simultaneous revivals on Broadway, matching Hammerstein's feat of six years earlier), giving testament to the enduring popularity of Richard Rodgers and the sound of his music.

Something Wonderful

A Celebration of Oscar Hammerstein II
on his 100th birthday

Wednesday, July 12, 1995
Gershwin Theatre, New York

SYNOPSIS

Gertrude Lawrence as Anna, with Sandy Kennedy as her son Louis, in the original 1951 Broadway production.

Act I opens with the arrival in Bangkok of a young English widow, Mrs. Anna Leonowens. The attractive and headstrong schoolteacher has been appointed to tutor the children of the King of Siam. Anna's son, Louis, has accompanied her on the journey, and she attempts to calm his fears—as well as her own apprehensions—with a song (**"I Whistle a Happy Tune"**).

Although Anna was expecting to have a house of her own, she is informed upon arrival that she will live in the royal palace instead. This does not sit well with her, but she agrees to reside in the palace for a short time until she can address the matter directly with the King.

Meanwhile, the King receives a gift from the Prince of Burma—a young woman named Tuptim. She is escorted by the courtier Lun Tha, and it is clear that a love affair has blossomed during the journey from their own country to Siam. The King accepts Tuptim with nonchalant gratitude, and Tuptim muses sadly about her circumstances (**"My Lord and Master"**).

"Royal Princess" Kelly Jordan Bit bows to her father, the King (Lou Diamond Phillips) while "Mrs. Anna" (Donna Murphy) looks on, in the 1996 Broadway revival.   Photo: Joan Marcus

Anna is introduced to the King, who turns a deaf ear to her complaint regarding accommodations. Lady Thiang, chief among the King's wives, counsels Anna on how things operate in the palace—the King is supreme and must never be questioned. Anna is deeply sympathetic to the plight of Tuptim and Lun Tha, who will never see each other again once Lun Tha returns to Burma (**"Hello, Young Lovers"**). The King's sixty-seven children are formally introduced to Anna by way of an impressive procession (**"The March of the Siamese Children"**).

Anna's Western approach to teaching begins to influence the King's inner thoughts, and he is unsure of what is best for his country and family (**"A Puzzlement"**). In the schoolroom, Anna is quickly developing a bond with her students (**"Getting to Know You"**), but her challenge lies in broadening their perspective, since they have never even seen a world map. The King is supportive of her efforts to modernize the education, but is still unwilling to provide Anna and her son with a house of their own. Anna protests firmly that she is being treated like a menial servant, and the King just as firmly reminds her that she is exactly that, and must behave accordingly. Meanwhile, Lun Tha and Tuptim have been meeting secretly in the palace garden (**"We Kiss in a Shadow"**).

Donna Murphy as Anna sings "Getting to Know You" with the Royal Children in the 1996 Broadway revival.
Photo: Joan Marcus

Anna vents her frustration in the privacy of her room (**"Shall I Tell You What I Think of You?"**). She cannot tolerate the King's stubborn disrespect any longer, and resolves that she must leave Siam before she grows too attached to the children. The King, however, is facing a bigger crisis. A letter to the British has been discovered, which describes the King as a barbarian, and suggests that Siam should be

Anna (Gertrude Lawrence) greets British envoy Sir Edward Ramsay (Robin Craven) as the King of Siam (Yul Brynner) looks on, in the original 1951 Broadway production.

annexed as a protectorate. Lady Thiang confides to Anna that—although he is too proud to admit it—the King needs her support and advice. As Anna listens to Lady Thiang pour out her love for this man (**"Something Wonderful"**), she decides to help him.

The King informs Anna that Sir Edward Ramsay, a British diplomat from Singapore, will be visiting Siam to assess the accusations of barbarism for himself. Anna suggests that the King should display his efforts toward "civilization" with a European dinner, ball and theatrical presentation—complete with European clothing for the women.

The grand event takes place as Act II begins. Despite the Eastern ladies' discomfort in their hoop skirts (**"Western People Funny"**), the evening's festivities are a success. Sir Edward can depart with confidence that the King of Siam is not a barbarian at all, but rather quite cultured. In the meantime, Lun Tha and Tuptim have made plans to run away together (**"I Have Dreamed"**).

Lawrence and Brynner, Broadway, 1951

The King is grateful to Anna for her assistance with the gala, and presents her with a ring from his own hand as a gift. Anna and the King discuss European customs, such as social dancing. Anna teaches the King how to dance as English couples do (**"Shall We Dance?"**), and they glide around the room together. The enchanting moment is broken, however, when Tuptim is suddenly brought before the King. She has been caught trying to escape with Lun Tha, who was killed during the attempt. The King prepares to whip the young girl, but Anna intercedes fiercely on her behalf. After stinging remarks from Anna implying that he has never loved and therefore cannot understand, the King flings down the whip and storms out.

Completely disillusioned, Anna decides to leave Siam once and for all. She returns the ring to the King via the Kralahome (Prime Minister), and plans to board the next boat out of Bangkok. But before she can leave, Lady Thiang delivers a letter from the King. He has fallen seriously ill, and in the letter Anna clearly sees the qualities she had once admired in him. She immediately goes to see him. The King is weak and dying, and he implores Anna to remain in Siam with his children. He will be succeeded by his son, Prince Chulalongkorn—a young man who will need guidance. Anna cannot find it in her heart to abandon the children she has grown to love, and she orders her baggage to be removed from the ship. The King dies with Anna kneeling at his side.

GETTING TO KNOW
THE KING AND I

There is some disagreement as to exactly how THE KING AND I came to be written. In his autobiography *Musical Stages*, Richard Rodgers wrote: "For the first time in our career, a project was submitted by someone who wanted to play the leading role, Gertrude Lawrence." Rodgers & Hammerstein historian David Ewen wrote: "Rodgers & Hammerstein's respective

Gertrude Lawrence, Broadway, 1951

wives read Margaret Landon's novel soon after its publication in 1944. They suggested it to their husbands for a musical play." Hugh Fordin in his biography of Oscar Hammerstein II says the idea was Fanny Holzman's, "the shrewd theatrical attorney" who represented Gertrude Lawrence. Lawrence's husband Richard Aldrich wrote in *Mrs. A* that "Gertrude and Fanny had made tentative plans... They had secured a composer, an exceedingly well-known one who had provided the score for one of Gertrude's big London hits." Sheridan Morley called the question in his biography of Lawrence when he wrote, "Gertie suggested Cole Porter, who seemed less than enthusiastic." And there is a first edition copy of

Anna and the King of Siam in the Rodgers & Hammerstein office with a note inside from the well-known agent Helen Strauss saying, "Bennett Cerf tells me he talked to you about [this book] as a possibility for a musical. Let me know what you think of the idea."

Wherever the idea actually came from, one thing is certain: THE KING AND I was written around and for the character of Anna Leonowens. Hers were the memoirs (two lengthy tomes), which were novelized by Margaret Landon into *Anna and the King of Siam*, which, in turn, inspired 20th Century Fox to make a movie in 1946 starring Irene Dunne and Rex Harrison. Then somehow among Fanny Holtzman, Gertrude Lawrence, Richard Rodgers and Oscar Hammerstein II, a musical was created for a star. Even its title reflected that focus: the third person title of Margaret Landon's novel *Anna and the King of Siam* was changed to the first person THE KING AND I. And when the show opened on Broadway in 1951, the original billing read: "Gertrude Lawrence in a New Musical Play THE KING AND I."

Since Rodgers & Hammerstein were attracted to love stories, it was clear from the outset that there would be a love story in THE KING AND I. But it was to be an innovative love story, to say the least, including clashing cultures and opposing traditions. Rodgers & Hammerstein were good at creating musicals in which opposites attract. They had already shown their ability to write for characters who, although obviously drawn to each other, cannot and do not express their feelings directly. Having written "People Will Say We're In Love" ["don't throw bouquets at me…"] for OKLAHOMA! and "If I Loved You" ["time and again I would try to say…"] for CAROUSEL, they were well equipped to handle the story of a schoolteacher and a king who have nothing in common.

Gertrude Lawrence and Yul Brynner, Broadway, 1951

"Shall We Dance?" Brynner and Lawrence, Broadway, 1951

At the end of the song, while he does not admit that he is convinced to any degree, it is apparent that he has found her very attractive and somehow can feel this illogical impulse himself, however vaguely."

The end result appears, at first glance, different from what Hammerstein conceived. The one song became two, her part doesn't "describe a romantic love," he doesn't present "logical arguments against sentimental monogamy," etc. And yet the finished scene, written in the third person ("…a young girl at her first dance…") creates a situation in which an innocent act of teaching a polka—surely one of the least romantic of all dances—becomes a statement of recognized passion. Clearly by the time this sequence was written Rodgers & Hammerstein felt the King's "illogical impulse" could be a bit less vague than originally intended. They also succeeded in capturing in this one brief sequence, the summation of a complicated relationship between a strong-minded man and an equally strong-minded woman. It's all there.

Original sheet music cover

The same early draft reveals another subtle but important difference. In the final playing version, it is clear that the King dies at the final curtain. But here is Hammerstein's original description of the scene:

"As Chulalongkorn continues, Anna has come closer to the King. She touches his hand. He does not stir. The music swells. Impulsively Anna sinks to her knees and kisses his hand. The smile has not left the King's face. Maybe he is only asleep—there is no way of telling. If his busy life has finished, he has left it with a sense of security for his people, for the new King, Chulalongkorn, has Anna."

Which brings us to the character of the King. Although he is listed first in the show's title, his role was intended to be the second lead. When Rodgers & Hammerstein were looking for someone to play the part, they first asked Rex Harrison. Noel Coward, Gertrude Lawrence's great friend and confidante, was discussed as a possibility as well. They then offered it to Alfred Drake, one of the stars of OKLAHOMA!,

Mrs. Anna is an employee who stands up for herself when she feels she must, which throws stumbling blocks in the way of any relationship between them. The King, however, is fascinated by her, but why is sometimes hard to fathom. That they become attracted to each other is clear, making for an irresistible, if challenging dramatic scenario.

A glimpse at an early pre-rehearsal script gives some insight into just how delicate the construction of the love story was. Here is the way Hammerstein described the "Shall We Dance?" scene, generally accepted as the apotheosis of the relationship between Mrs. Anna and the King of Siam:

"Anna tries to explain the Western idea of the love of one man for one woman. It will introduce a new song, which will be Anna's attempt to describe a romantic love totally foreign to the King's idea of relations between man and woman. In his part of the song his logical arguments against sentimental monogamy must be a difficult one for Anna to answer. She can only fall back on the fact that in the Western world, this thing which seems so foolish and impossible to him is happening every hour of the day, every day, and a man and a girl are falling in love, believing that they are the only people in the world for each other.

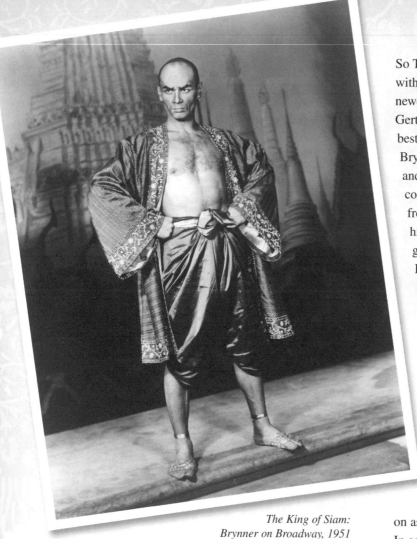

The King of Siam:
Brynner on Broadway, 1951

So THE KING AND I opened on Broadway in 1951 with a genuine star as Mrs. Anna and a dynamic newcomer as the King. Both Yul Brynner and Gertrude Lawrence won Tony Awards that year; he as best featured actor and she as best leading actress. Brynner played the King in the 1956 movie version and won the Oscar for best actor. While his career continued with success, he could never get too far from the King of Siam. The role all but overtook him. A short summer stock run in the mid-1970s grew into a series of successful engagements on Broadway (twice), London and across the U.S. essentially until the end of his life. From being known originally as THE KING AND *I*, the show had become THE *KING* AND I. By the time Brynner gave his 4,625th and final performance in New York, the actress playing Mrs. Anna was neither mentioned nor pictured on the marquee of the theater. And to come full circle, she was nominated for a Tony Award as best featured actress.

Ultimately, the musical that was conceived by one star, and made a star out of another, has transcended its star vehicle status to live on as a classic in its own right with two starring roles. In addition to the legendary Gertrude Lawrence and Yul Brynner, a host of great names have played these star parts over the years. The honor roll includes, as Anna: Elaine Paige, Donna Murphy, Hayley Mills, Susan Hampshire, Angela Lansbury, Barbara Cook, Jan Clayton, Jeannette MacDonald, Betsy Palmer, Eileen Brennan, Betty White, Virginia McKenna and Florence Henderson. The King, meanwhile, has been played by, among others: Lou Diamond Phillips, Darren McGavin, Alfred Drake, Cameron Mitchell, Farley Granger, Ricardo Montalban, Pernell Roberts, Theodore Bikel, Stacey Keach and Rudolf Nureyev.

In 1992 Philips Classics released a studio cast recording of THE KING AND I. Under the baton of John Mauceri and featuring the Hollywood Bowl Orchestra, the all-star recording was led by Julie Andrews (Anna) and Ben Kingsley (The King), with Lea Salonga (Tuptim), Peabo Bryson (Lun Tha), Marilyn Horne (Lady Thiang) and cameo appearances by Martin Sheen and Roger Moore.

who turned them down. After several other tries they did find someone: a man who had retired from acting and was directing for CBS Television. Persuaded to audition by Mary Martin, he came out on the stage, and, as Richard Rodgers described, "scowled, plunked one whacking chord on his guitar and began to howl in a strange language that no one could understand." The search for the King was over. The man was Yul Brynner.

Earlier that season, a new production starring Hayley Mills began touring Australia. Distinctive and unusual, this production caught the eye of composer Rodgers' daughter Mary, who declared it the best KING AND I she had ever seen. Within a short time

"Western People Funny"   Anna (Gertrude Lawrence) and the
King's wives prepare for a Royal Banquet, in a scene from the
1951 Broadway production.

Lou Diamond Phillips and Donna Murphy from the 1996 Broadway revival   Photo: Joan Marcus

the wheels were set in motion to bring this production 10,000 miles up to Broadway. It arrived four years later, opening at the Neil Simon Theatre on April 11, 1996, starring Tony Award winner Donna Murphy as Anna and film star Lou Diamond Phillips as the King. Hailed by the critics and public alike, THE KING AND I swept the triple crown of Broadway honors that spring, winning the Tony Award, Drama Desk Award and Outer Critics' Circle Awards for Best Musical Revival. A U.S. National Tour, starring Hayley Mills for its first year, opened in Minneapolis in April of 1997; a London version of this production, starring Elaine Paige, opened at the legendary Palladium in May of 2000, where it played for nearly two years.

Today, THE KING AND I still reigns, its majesty still shines. Since the very beginning it has been a favorite of all kinds of theaters around the world. High school students have shaved their heads, struggled with hoop skirts and studied basic Asian dance postures. Dinner theaters have cleared away the dessert dishes only moments before Mrs. Anna's boat arrived in Bangkok. In Germany, it reigns as DER KONIG UND ICH, in Israel as HA'MELEKH V'ANI, and in France with the poetic title LE ROI ET MOI.

In 1956 Oscar Hammerstein II attended a charity screening of the film version in Australia. He then wrote to his partner, Richard Rodgers: "I am convinced that this is our best work. I have a kind of humble feeling of not knowing how we did it. It has more wisdom as well as heart than any other musical play by anybody. It will remain 'modern' long after any of our other plays."

Theodore S. Chapin
President, The Rodgers & Hammerstein Organization
Fall 2006

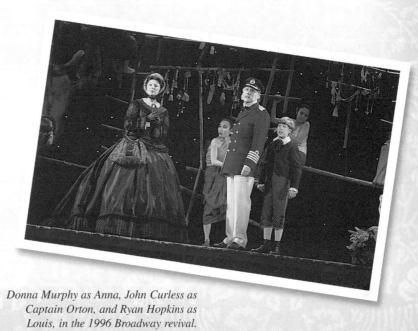

Donna Murphy as Anna, John Curless as
Captain Orton, and Ryan Hopkins as
Louis, in the 1996 Broadway revival.
Photo: Joan Marcus

GETTING TO KNOW YOU

Lyrics by OSCAR HAMMERSTEIN II

Music by RICHARD RODGERS

It's a ver-y an-cient say-ing But a true and hon-est thought, That if you be-come a teach-er, by your pu-pils you'll be taught. As a teach-er, I've been

HELLO, YOUNG LOVERS

Lyrics by OSCAR HAMMERSTEIN II

Music by RICHARD RODGERS

I HAVE DREAMED

Lyrics by OSCAR HAMMERSTEIN II

Music by RICHARD RODGERS

I WHISTLE A HAPPY TUNE

Lyrics by OSCAR HAMMERSTEIN II

Music by RICHARD RODGERS

are.   *Whistle*

You may be as

brave   as   you   make   be - lieve   you

are.

THE MARCH OF THE SIAMESE CHILDREN

Music by RICHARD RODGERS

Deliberately

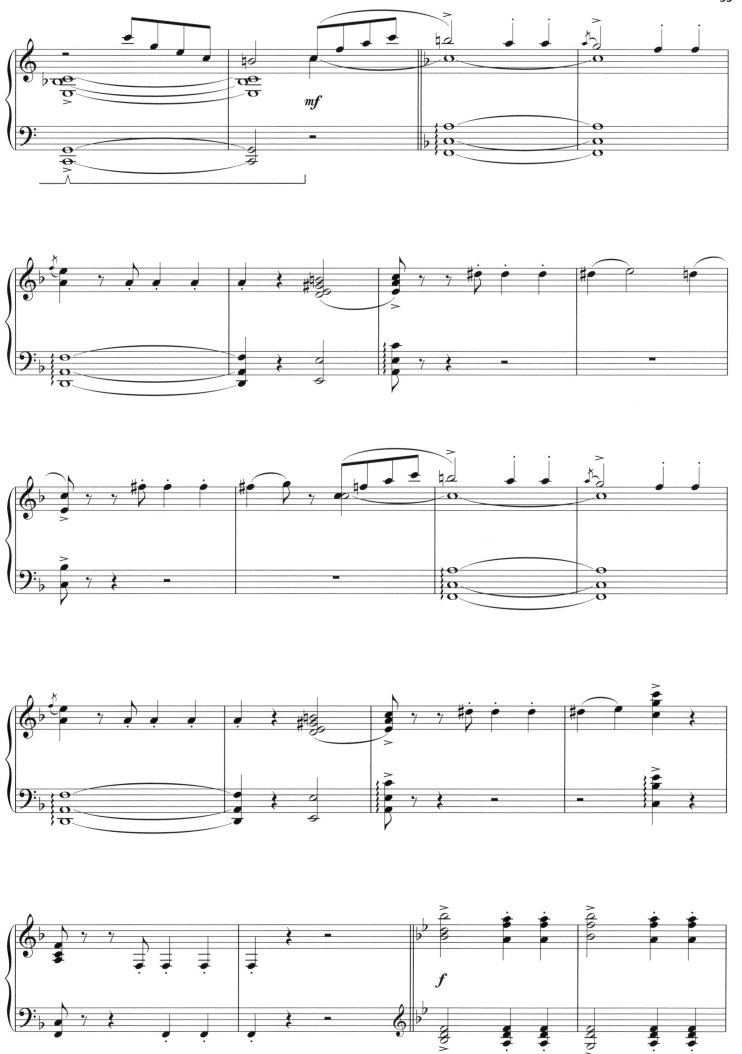

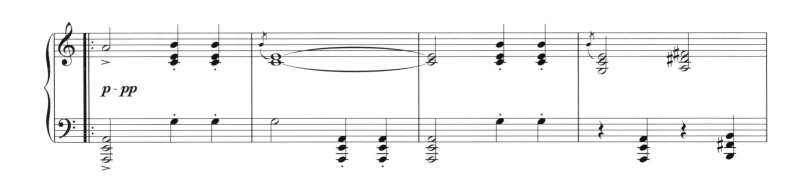

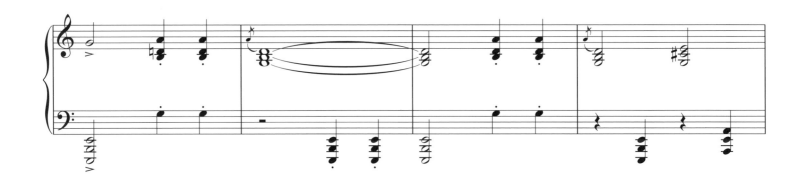

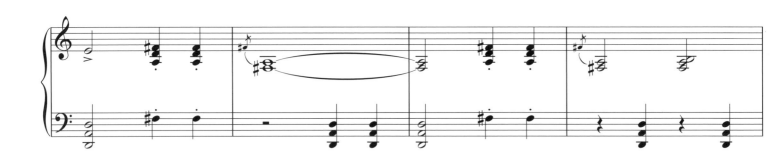

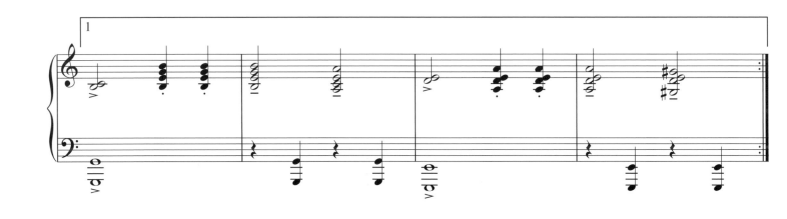

MY LORD AND MASTER

Lyrics by OSCAR HAMMERSTEIN II

Music by RICHARD RODGERS

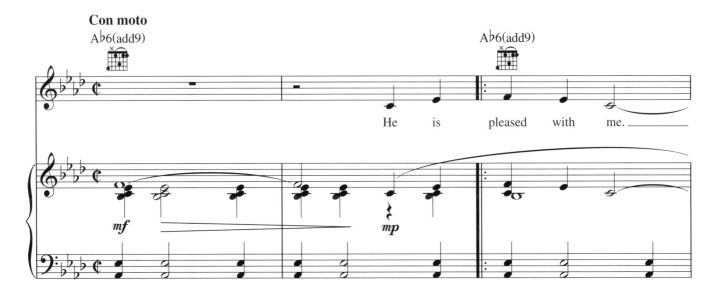

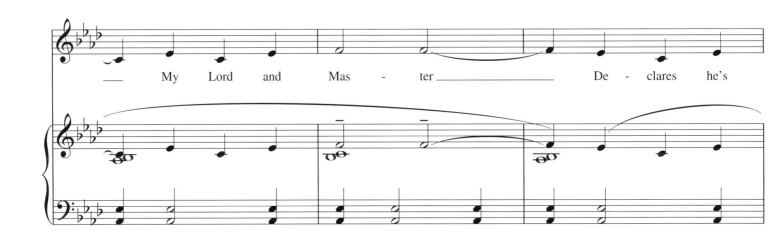

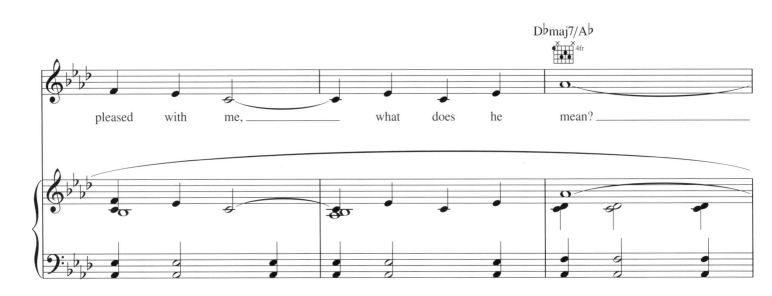

WESTERN PEOPLE FUNNY

Lyrics by OSCAR HAMMERSTEIN II

Music by RICHARD RODGERS

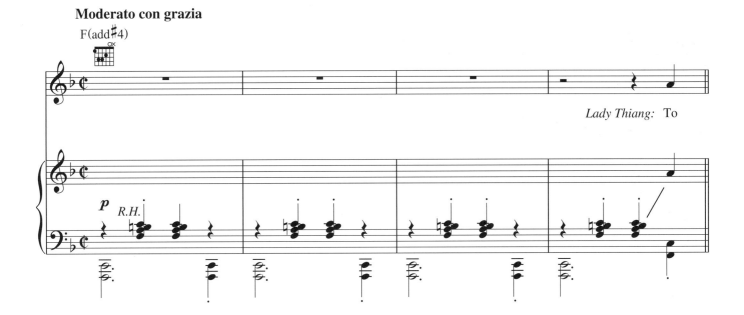

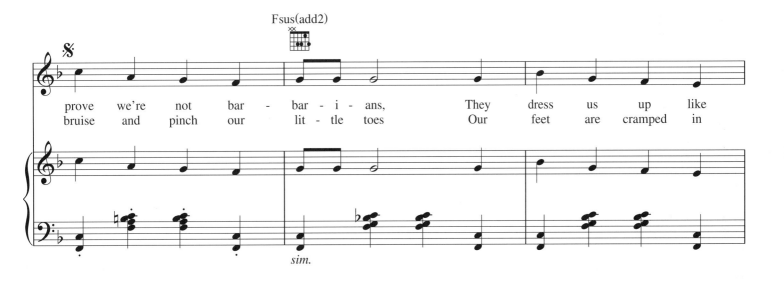

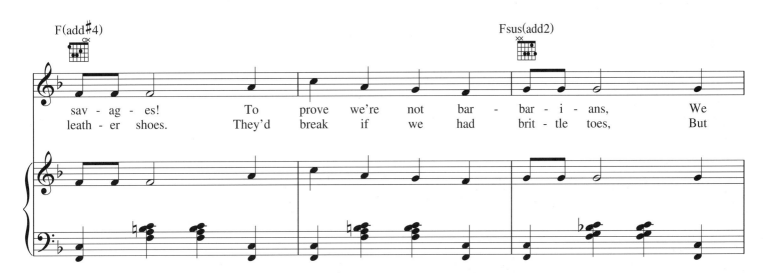

A PUZZLEMENT

Lyrics by OSCAR HAMMERSTEIN II

Music by RICHARD RODGERS

Vivace ma non troppo

times I al-most think I am not sure of what I ab-so-lute-ly know.
fa-ther was a king He was a king who knew ex-act-ly what he knew,
times I al-most think no-bod-y sure of what he ab-so-lute-ly know,

Ver-y of-ten find con-fu-sion in con-
And his brain was not a thing For-ev-er
Ev-'ry-bod-y find con-fu-sion in con-

clu-sion I con-clud-ed long a-go.
swing-ing to and fro and fro and to.
clu-sion he con-clud-ed long a-go.

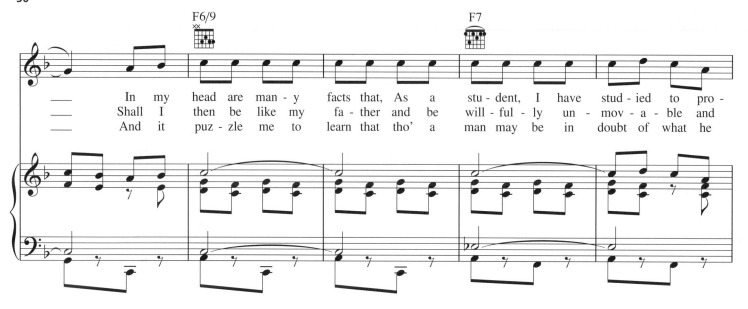

In my head are man - y facts that, As a stu - dent, I have stud - ied to pro -
Shall I then be like my fa - ther and be will - ful - ly un - mov - a - ble and
And it puz - zle me to learn that tho' a man may be in doubt of what he

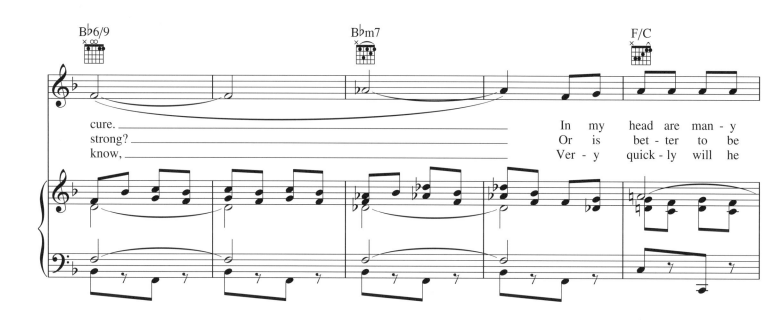

cure. _____
strong? _____
know, _____

In my head are man - y
Or is bet - ter to be
Ver - y quick - ly will he

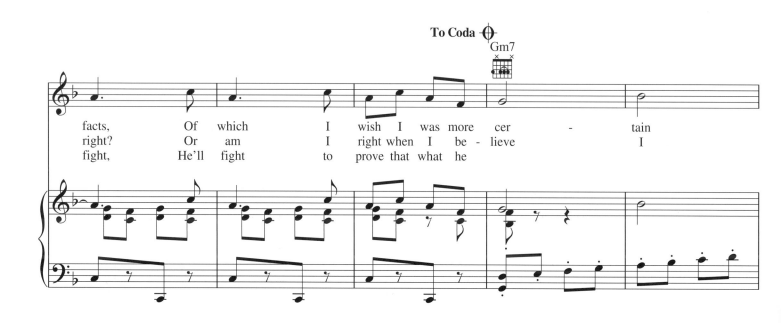

facts, Of which I wish I was more cer - tain
right? Or am I right when I be - lieve I
fight, He'll fight to prove that what he

To Coda ⊕

SHALL I TELL YOU WHAT I THINK OF YOU?

Lyrics by OSCAR HAMMERSTEIN II

Music by RICHARD RODGERS

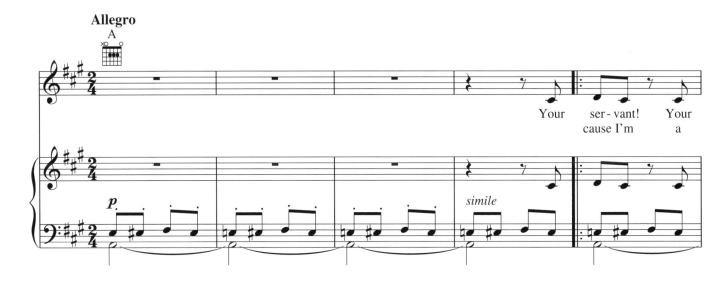

Your ser - vant! Your
cause I'm a

ser - vant! In - deed I'm not your ser - vant (al - though you give me less than ser - vant's
wom - an, You think like ev - 'ry wom - an I have to be a slave or con - cu -

pay.) _____ I'm a free and in - de - pen - dent em - ploy -
bine. _____ You con - ceit - ed, self - in - dul - gent lib - er -

SHALL WE DANCE?

Lyrics by OSCAR HAMMERSTEIN II

Music by RICHARD RODGERS

Brightly (*moderato*)

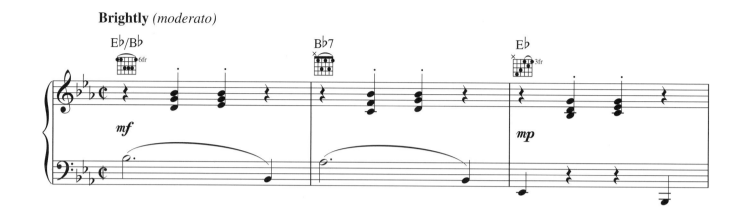

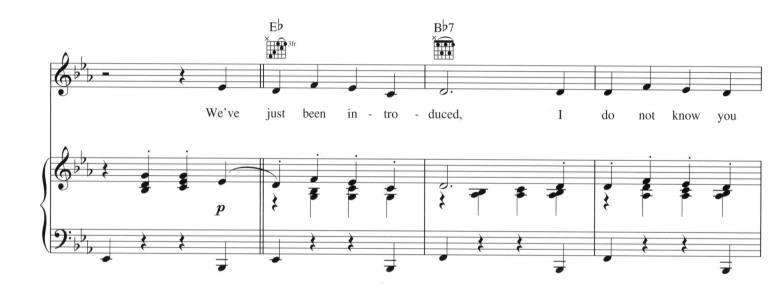

We've just been in-tro-duced, I do not know you

well. But when the mu-sic start-ed, some-thing drew me to your side. So

SOMETHING WONDERFUL

Lyrics by OSCAR HAMMERSTEIN II

Music by RICHARD RODGERS

The thought-less things he'll do will hurt and wor-ry you

Then, all at once, he'll do some-thing won-der-ful. He

has a thou-sand dreams that won't come true. You

più espressivo

know that he be-lieves in them And that's e-nough for you.

cresc. *mf*

WE KISS IN A SHADOW

Lyrics by OSCAR HAMMERSTEIN II

Music by RICHARD RODGERS

Molto moderato e semplice

Refrain *(slowly and tenderly)*

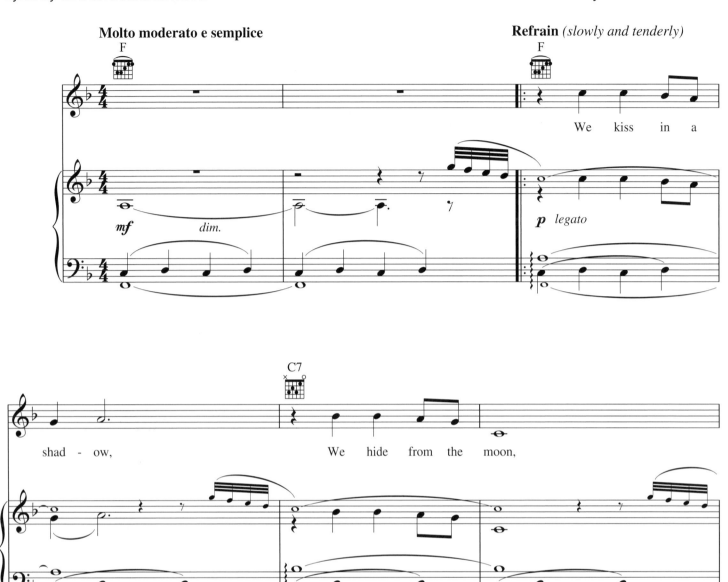

We kiss in a shad-ow,

We hide from the moon,

Our meet-ings are few and o-ver too soon.

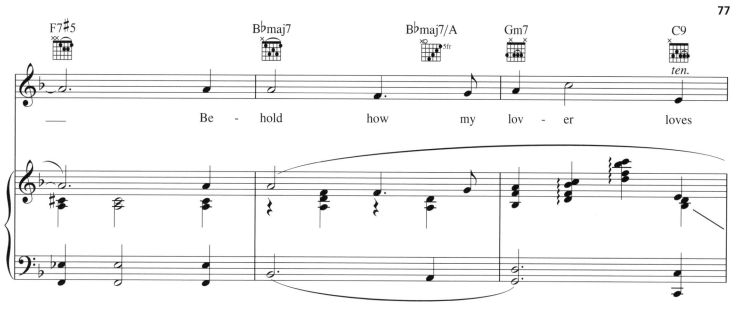

Be - hold how my lov - er loves

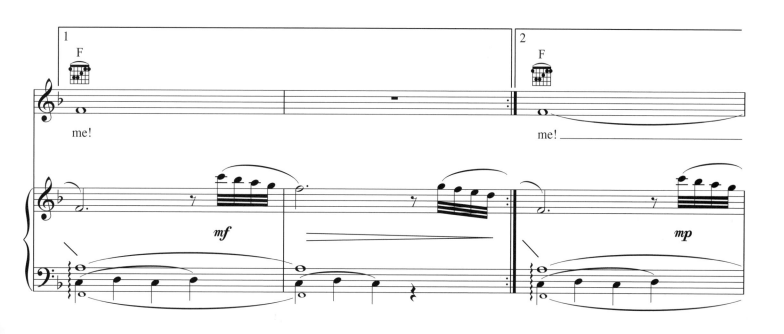

me!

me!

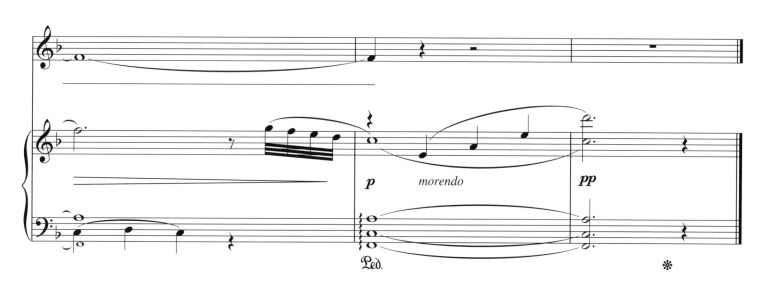

RODGERS AND HAMMERSTEIN™
VOCAL SELECTIONS

ALLEGRO
HL00312007 . . . .$10.95
Come Home • A Fellow Needs a Girl • The Gentleman Is a Dope • Money Isn't Ev'rything • So Far • You Are Never Away

CAROUSEL
HL01121008 . . . .$14.95
Blow High, Blow Low • The Carousel Waltz • Geraniums in the Winder • The Highest Judge of All • If I Loved You • June Is Bustin' Out All Over • Mister Snow • A Real Nice Clambake • Soliloquy • What's the Use of Wond'rin' • When the Children Are Asleep • You'll Never Walk Alone

CINDERELLA
HL00312091 . . . .$14.95
Boys and Girls Like You and Me • Cinderella March • Cinderella Waltz • Do I Love You Because You're Beautiful? • Falling in Love with Love • Impossible • In My Own Little Corner • Loneliness of Evening • A Lovely Night • Stepsisters' Lament • The Sweetest Sounds • Ten Minutes Ago • There's Music in You

FLOWER DRUM SONG
HL00312140 . . . .$14.95
Chop Suey • Don't Marry Me • Fan Tan Fannie • Grant Avenue • A Hundred Million Miracles • I Am Going to Like It Here • I Enjoy Being a Girl • Like a God • Love, Look Away • My Best Love • The Other Generation • Sunday • You Are Beautiful

THE KING AND I
HL00312227 . . . .$14.95
Getting to Know You • Hello, Young Lovers • I Have Dreamed • I Whistle a Happy Tune • The March of the Siamese Children • My Lord and Master • A Puzzlement • Shall I Tell You What I Think of You? • Shall We Dance? • Something Wonderful • We Kiss in a Shadow • Western People Funny

ME AND JULIET
HL00312256 . . . .$10.95
The Big Black Giant • I'm Your Girl • It's Me • Keep It Gay • Marriage Type Love • No Other Love • That's the Way It Happens • A Very Special Day

OKLAHOMA!
HL00312292 . . . .$14.95
All Er Nothin' • The Farmer and the Cowman • I Cain't Say No • Kansas City • Lonely Room • Many a New Day • Oh, What a Beautiful Mornin' • Oklahoma • Out of My Dreams • People Will Say We're in Love • Pore Jud • The Surrey with the Fringe on Top

PIPE DREAM
HL00312320 . . . .$10.95
All at Once You Love Her • All Kinds of People • Everybody's Got a Home But Me • The Man I Used to Be • The Next Time It Happens • Suzy Is a Good Thing • Sweet Thursday

THE SOUND OF MUSIC
HL00312392 . . . .$14.95
Climb Ev'ry Mountain • Do-Re-Mi • Edelweiss • I Have Confidence • The Lonely Goatherd • Maria • My Favorite Things • An Ordinary Couple • Sixteen Going On Seventeen • So Long, Farewell • Something Good • The Sound of Music • Wedding Processional

SOUTH PACIFIC
HL00312400 . . . .$14.95
Bali Ha'i • Bloody Mary • A Cock-Eyed Optimist • Dites-Moi (Tell Me Why) • Happy Talk • Honey Bun • I'm Gonna Wash That Man Right Outa My Hair • My Girl Back Home • Some Enchanted Evening • There Is Nothin' Like a Dame • This Nearly Was Mine • Twin Soliloquies (This Is How It Feels) • A Wonderful Guy • You've Got to Be Carefully Taught • Younger Than Springtime

STATE FAIR
HL00312403 . . . .$14.95
All I Owe Ioway • Boys and Girls Like You and Me • Isn't It Kinda Fun • It Might As Well Be Spring • It's a Grand Night for Singing • It's the Little Things in Texas • The Man I Used to Be • More Than Just a Friend • Never Say "No" • The Next Time It Happens • Our State Fair • So Far • That's for Me • That's the Way It Happens • This Isn't Heaven • When I Go Out Walking with My Baby • Willing and Eager • You Never Had It So Good

Prices, contents and availability subject to change without notice.

FOR MORE INFORMATION, SEE YOUR LOCAL MUSIC DEALER, OR WRITE TO:

HAL•LEONARD®
CORPORATION
7777 W. BLUEMOUND RD. P.O. BOX 13819 MILWAUKEE, WI 53213